# PICASSO: SCULPTOR/PAINTER

SIMON WILSON

# Picasso: Sculptor/Painter
## A BRIEF GUIDE

TATE GALLERY

Exhibition sponsored by

**ℨ ERNST & YOUNG**

Ernst & Young is an award winner under the Business Sponsorship Incentive Scheme for its support of the *Picasso: Sculptor/Painter* exhibition. The BSIS is a Government Scheme administered by ABSA (Association for Business Sponsorship of the Arts).

*cover*
**Little Owl** 1951–2 (no.123)

*frontispiece*
La Californie, Cannes 1957
Photo: David Douglas Duncan

ISBN 1 85437 135 5

Published by order of the Trustees 1994
for the exhibition at the Tate Gallery 16 February – 8 May 1994
Published by Tate Gallery Publications, Millbank, London SW1P 4RG
Reprinted with corrections 1994
Designed by Caroline Johnston
© Tate Gallery 1994 All rights reserved
Typeset in Monotype Columbus by ICON Colour, London
and Tate Gallery Publications
Printed in Great Britain on 150gsm Parilux Matt White
by Balding + Mansell, Wisbech, Cambridgeshire
All works by Pablo Picasso © DACS 1994

# Contents

# Sponsor's Foreword

Ernst & Young is delighted to be sponsoring the Tate Gallery's major exhibition, *Picasso: Sculptor/Painter*.

Picasso's vision and originality find many echoes in the philosophy of Ernst & Young. He gained his reputation by breaking down barriers and setting new standards for others to follow. Internationally he was a leader and a visionary. At Ernst & Young we pursue the same principles of leadership, vision and originality of thought for the benefit of our clients. Like Picasso, we aim to be always at the leading edge.

As one of the largest firms of business and financial advisers in the world, we welcome the opportunity to contribute to the cultural life of the countries in which we operate. Through its exhibitions and educational projects, the Tate Gallery makes a major contribution to cultural life in the United Kingdom and our sponsorship of *Picasso: Sculptor/Painter* is one way that we can help it maintain the very high standards that its visitors have come to expect.

We hope that you will enjoy this unique exhibition and that this book will provide a reminder for the years to come.

Elwyn Eilledge
*Senior Partner*

# Foreword

This is the fourth Picasso exhibition to be held at the Tate Gallery. The first was the legendary exhibition of 1960. Then, in 1967, Roland Penrose presented one of the first exhibitions devoted solely to Picasso's sculpture. Finally, in 1988, we mounted *Late Picasso: Paintings, Sculpture, Drawings, Prints 1953–1972*.

We were delighted when in 1991 both John Golding and Elizabeth Cowling accepted our invitation to work together to realise the current exhibition. Not only did they select the works but also have produced a detailed catalogue in which every work exhibited is reproduced in colour.

However, in order to reach as wide a public as possible we have decided to publish this short well-illustrated introduction, written by Simon Wilson and based on the material in the full catalogue, which provides a guide to each of the eight sections of the exhibition.

The exhibition would not have been possible without the generous support of our many lenders, both public collections and private collections from all over the world. We are deeply grateful to them all for their enthusiasm for the project. Our special thanks go to Claude Ruiz-Picasso and other members of the Picasso family as well as to the Musée Picasso and the Musée National d'Art Moderne in Paris and to the Museum of Modern Art in New York.

We believe that the exhibition will offer all visitors a wider knowledge of Picasso's work and a greater understanding of his creative spirit.

The exhibition could not have been realised without the sponsorship of Ernst & Young. Their involvement in the project and their considerable interest and enthusiasm are sincerely appreciated.

Nicholas Serota
*Director*

# Author's Note

This book is intended as a guide to the exhibition *Picasso: Sculptor/Painter* as well as a souvenir of it. The sections of the book correspond to the sections of the exhibition and all works discussed in the text are given their exhibition number as well as their plate number in the book, if they are illustrated. All the illustrations are given their exhibition number as well as their plate number (the abbreviation 'no.' indicates the exhibition number; 'pl.' refers to the colour plate). The text is based on the scholarly texts in the exhibition catalogue by John Golding and Elizabeth Cowling

    Measurements are given in centimetres; height before width, followed by depth where appropriate.

# Introduction

Picasso is acknowledged as one of the great revolutionary modern painters. Less widely appreciated is the fact that he was equally revolutionary and influential as a sculptor.

In his lifetime Picasso created a huge body of sculptural work but it was little seen until he was persuaded to include a large group of sculptures in his great retrospective in Paris in 1966. The following year these were shown at the Tate Gallery and then at the Museum of Modern Art, New York. Picasso's sculpture came as a revelation, and was greeted with acclaim in all three venues.

Now the Tate Gallery has created an exhibition which both presents Picasso's sculpture to a new generation and makes the first attempt to relate it to his painting. The exhibition sets out to show how Picasso's sculpture was nourished by his work in two dimensions, but, more surprisingly, also how his sculpture often fed back into his painting, altering and enriching it.

Even more than his painting, Picasso's sculpture reveals his extraordinary inventiveness and originality – both in his use of materials and in his continual transformations of reality into new and compelling forms of art. In his Cubist collages and constructions he established the idea that art could be made from any materials the artist chooses and that sculpture could be constructed, rather than carved or modelled. In his art generally he established that reality may be treated in art in any way the artist pleases. These principles have had an enormous influence on subsequent art. In particular many of the most radical forms of modern sculpture have their origins in the work of Picasso.

Picasso's sculptures had a special importance for him: he parted with few in his lifetime and then with reluctance. His paintings he always sold much more freely. It is partly for this reason that the sculpture remained for so long so relatively little known and so critically disregarded.

# 1 Crisis and Analysis

Picasso made his first sculpture in 1902 but it was not until 1906 that he seriously turned his attention to the medium, precipitating what can be seen as a sculptural crisis in his painting. This was the time of his first important love affair, with the Parisian model Fernande Olivier. Hers is the 'Head of a Woman' (cat.no.1; pl.1) that Picasso modelled in clay (later cast in bronze) probably in the spring of 1906. He spent the summer with Fernande at the remote and primitive village of Gósol in the Pyrenees. There he painted a group of sensual and serene figure pictures, mostly nudes, which lie at the heart of his Rose Period. They are suffused with the pink and ochre colours of the earth of Gósol itself. On their return to Paris he continued in this vein with works such as 'Two Nudes' (cat.no.9; pl.2) and 'Seated Nude with Crossed Legs' (cat.no.10; pl.3). But the figures in these paintings now have an exaggerated solidity that is highly sculptural, and 'Two Nudes' is in fact one figure seen from two points of view. Picasso was becoming dissatisfied with the conventions of Western painting and was turning increasingly to sculptural sources in his search for an alternative. For example, the stylised faces of the 'Two Nudes' reflect his enthusiasm for Iberian sculpture. Examples of this archaic art had recently been uncovered and acquired by the Louvre.

In 1906–7 Picasso discovered tribal art. He later said 'At that moment I realised what painting was all about', a remark which shows how closely painting and sculpture were associated in his mind. In 1907–8 he produced a group of vigorously, even crudely chiselled wood carvings which reflect this discovery. Among them are 'Figure' (cat.no.4; pl.5) and 'Standing Man' (cat.no.3; pl.4). This first of these may be unfinished. The sculptural quality of his painting intensified in 1908 in works such as the pair 'Nude with Raised Arms' and 'Standing Nude' (cat.nos.11, 12) and 'Seated Nude' (cat.no.13; pl.6). In the last of these the sculptural angularity is combined with an eroticism which indicates Fernande's continuing presence in Picasso's work. Paintings such as this are so close to sculpture that Picasso famously remarked of them 'it would have been sufficient to cut them up … and reassemble them according to the indications given by the colour in order to be confronted with a sculpture'.

By the following year, 1909, Picasso, together with Georges Braque, had invented Cubism, a kind of painting more sculptural than any before, since it presented simultaneously more than one view of the subject (cat.nos.16–18; pl.7). Early Cubist painting is often referred to as 'Analytic'. This term reflects

Picasso in the Bateau Lavoir
(his studio from 1904–9) 1908
*Musée Picasso Archive, Paris*
Photo: Gelett Burgess

the idea that in those works Picasso began with a relatively recognisable object or figure and 'analysed' it – took it apart and restructured it – often to the point of abstraction. The faceting of the image typical of Analytical Cubist painting is seen in Picasso's sculptural 'Head of a Woman (Fernande)' of 1909, for long his best-known sculpture through the numerous bronzes of it cast by his dealer Vollard. One of these is shown here alongside one of two original plaster casts of the clay model (cat.nos.5, 6; pl.8). But Picasso realised that this work, however compelling, was essentially traditional: 'It was pointless to go on with this kind of sculpture', he said. Instead, the lessons of Cubist painting, that the parts of the subject could be freely moved and recombined in space, were about to be applied back to sculpture, and a revolution was on hand.

PLATE I
**Head of a Woman (Fernande)**
1906  36 × 24 × 23  (cat.no.1)

PLATE 2
**Two Nudes** 1906
151.3 × 93 (cat.no.9)

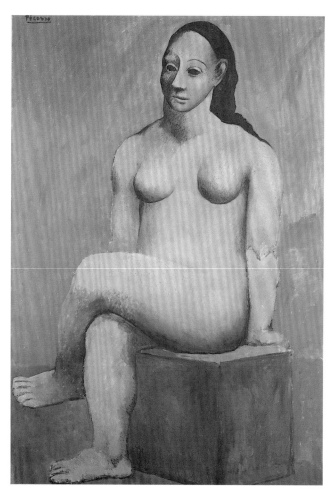

PLATE 3
**Seated Nude with Crossed Legs**
1906 151 × 100 (cat.no.10)

PLATE 4
**Standing Man** 1907 or 1908
37 × 6 × 6 (cat.no.3)

PLATE 5
**Figure** ?1908
80.5 × 24 × 20.8 (cat.no.4)

PLATE 6
**Seated Nude** 1908
150 × 100 (cat.no.13)

PLATE 7
**Seated Woman** 1909
81 × 65 (cat.no.17)

PLATE 8
**Head of a Woman
(Fernande)** 1909
41.9 × 26.1 × 26.7
(cat.no.6)

# 2  Construction and Synthesis

From the autumn of 1912 Picasso seems to have reversed the process of analysis in his Cubist works. He began to make collages and sculptures in which a representation of a real object or group of objects is constructed or assembled from disparate elements such as cardboard, many different kinds of paper, or scraps of wood, freely combined with drawing and painting. This process of bringing together gave rise to the term 'Synthetic' to describe this phase of Cubism, and the three-dimensional works are known as Cubist constructions. This section of the exhibition shows how Picasso began almost simultaneously to make Cubist collages and constructions and how these in turn affected his painting. An important point is how intimately the processes of collage and construction are related, dissolving the barriers between pictorial and sculptural art in an unprecedented way. A key work is the famous 'Guitar' (cat.no.19; pl.10) made first in cardboard in autumn 1912 and later given more permanent form in metal by Picasso. This, and the collages and constructions that followed, introduced a completely new way of making sculpture. Instead of sculpting the solid mass of the object Picasso presents its spaces, its surfaces, and its contours, playing games with different ways of representing the parts, and with their relationships, challenging and teasing the spectator. 'Guitar' for example is famous not least for the way in which the sound-hole of the instrument is defined as a tube of space. 'Musical Score and Guitar' (cat.no.27; pl.9) is a collage made about the same time as 'Guitar'. The body of the guitar is represented both vertically and horizontally using different coloured papers. The tilted white shape is the neck, and the bit of paper with two black bars presumably represents the frets. It is simply pinned on, emphasising the sculptural, constructed nature even of two-dimensional collage.

In the construction 'Still Life' 1914 (cat.no.22; pl.11) the glass is seen from the outside but is simultaneously opened up to reveal the inside with the level of liquid represented by the tilted wedge shape. The tablecloth is represented by a real bit of fringing. This work relates closely to the painting 'Glass, Newspaper and Bottle' (cat.no.36; pl.12) and by this time the interchange between Picasso's sculpture and painting was so fluid that it is impossible to guess which came first. In the same year Picasso made a fully in the round sculpture of a glass, the 'Glass of Absinthe' that is another of his most famous works. Six bronze casts were made from his original wax model. Each was then decorated differently by Picasso and equipped with a real silver-plate absinthe spoon and a simulated

Picasso in his studio,
rue Schoelcher, Paris c.1914
*Musée Picasso Archive, Paris*

sugar lump in bronze. Two of the six are in the exhibition (cat.nos.23, 24; pl.13). Again, the glass is opened up to reveal its interior and games are played with its parts and their relationships. It has been suggested that in his treatment of the glass Picasso was evoking the effects of being drunk, and also that the sculpture can be seen as a head with a hat. The 'Glass of Absinthe' has its pictorial counterpart in a group of exquisite small collages in which the focus is on a single glass or goblet. One of these is 'Bottle of Bass, Wineglass, Packet of Tobacco, Calling Card' (cat.no.33; pl.14).

Picasso's Cubist constructions reached a climax in 1915 with the huge painted metal 'Violin' (cat.no.26; pl.15). This belongs to a phase of Cubism sometimes called 'Rococo' from its decorative, light-hearted and colourful character. A related painting is 'Woman with a Guitar' (cat.no.37; pl.16).

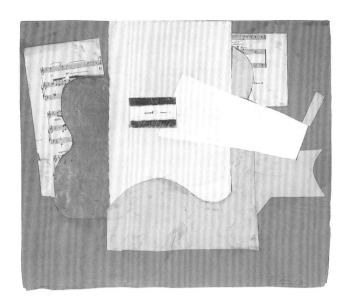

PLATE 9
**Musical Score and Guitar** 1912
42.5 × 48 (cat.no.27)

PLATE 10
**Guitar** ?1912–13
77.5 × 35 × 19.3
(cat.no.19)

PLATE 11
**Still Life** 1914
25.4 × 45.7 × 9.2 (cat.no.22)

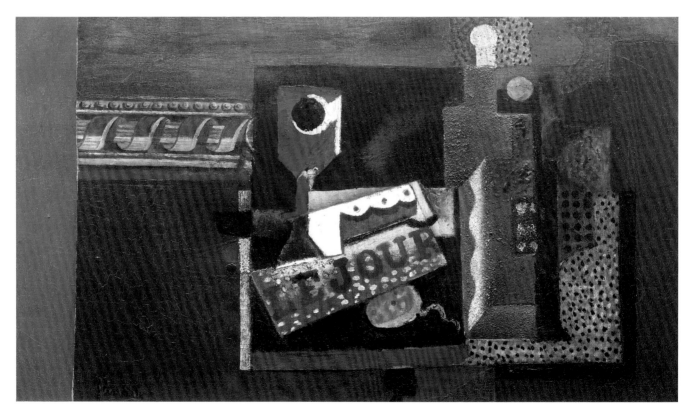

PLATE 12
**Glass, Newspaper and Bottle**
1914 36.2 × 61.3 (cat.no.36)

PLATE 13
**Glass of Absinthe** 1914
22 × 16.5 × 5 (cat.no.24)

PLATE 14
**Bottle of Bass, Wineglass, Packet of Tobacco, Calling Card** 1914
24 × 30.5 (cat.no.33)

PLATE 15
**Violin** 1915
100 × 63 × 18 (cat.no.26)

PLATE 16
**Woman with a Guitar** 1915
186 × 75 (cat.no.37)

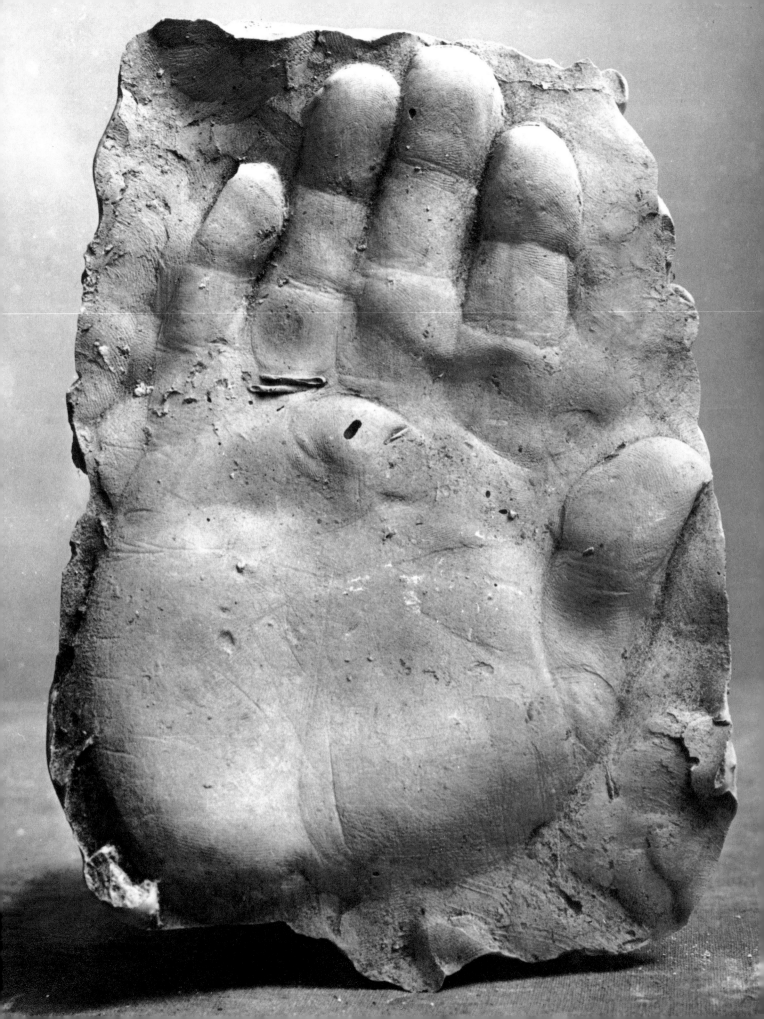

# 3 The Sculptor's Studio

This section focuses on the role of drawing in Picasso's sculptural thinking in the years from 1906 to 1936. The works in it relate therefore to both the preceding and the following sections. Many of Picasso's drawings over these years give the impression of being ideas or projects for sculptures that were never executed – they give us a glimpse of what might have been.

The powerful drawing 'Standing Nudes and Study of a Foot' (cat.no.50; pl.17) clearly relates to his wood carvings of 1907–8 (cat.nos.3, 4; pls.4, 5) and the heavily faceted 'Head of a Man' 1909 (cat.no.52) to the famous 'Head of a Woman (Fernande)' of 1909 (cat.nos.5, 6; pl.8). The great 1912 construction 'Guitar' (cat.no.19; pl.10) and what followed were heralded by scores of drawings. In 'Violin' 1912 (cat.no.54; pl.19) the instrument is shown hanging on the wall of the studio, which is how Picasso displayed both the musical instruments he owned and his constructions. The violin was the subject of one of the earliest of these as well as the later painted 'Violin' 1915 (cat.no.26; pl.15). Some of these drawings, for example 'Still Life: The Cruet Set' (cat.no.53; pl.18) clearly suggest fully three-dimensional sculptures.

On holiday in Saint-Raphaël in 1919 Picasso painted a striking gouache of a still life in front of a window (cat.no.60). The still life on the table is so vividly rendered as to look exactly like a pop-up paper construction, and on his return to Paris in the autumn Picasso made a number of paper sculptures, one of which is 'Guitar and Table in Front of a Window' (cat.no.39). This work belongs to a period, from 1915 to 1928, when Picasso made relatively little sculpture. From 1921 to 1924 he made none at all. In precisely these years however, he entered his neo-classical phase in which his paintings and drawings became peopled with enormously solid, giant figures inspired by the classical sculptural tradition. The figures in his 1921 pastel 'Three Nudes by the Sea' (cat.no.62; pl.20) are grouped and drawn to look exactly like a sculptured monument.

Picasso's mood of neo-classical calm changed abruptly in 1925, partly perhaps as a result of the serious deterioration of his relationship with his first wife Olga, a Russian ballerina he married in 1918. In 1927 and 1928 he produced a large number of bizarre and disturbing drawings in which the human figure is rendered in simplified forms, sometimes swollen and tumescent, sometimes bone-like. All remain intensely sculptural and 'Bathers (Study for Monument)' (cat.no.63; pl.21) is explicitly so. It is one of a whole group of drawings and sculptures relating to a monument Picasso had been commissioned to make for

Plaster cast of Picasso's hand 1937
Photo: Brassaï © Gilberte Brassaï

the tomb of his friend the poet and critic Guillaume Apollinaire who had died in the great flu epidemic of 1918 (see nos.73–6, 83; pls.28, 30, 31).

Many of the drawings of tumescent or bone-like structures appear in an extraordinary sketchbook which Picasso started and largely filled at the resort of Dinard in the summer of 1928. But alongside them are drawings of open, wire structures which announce a completely new phase of Picasso's sculpture and one of immense significance for later sculptors. Ten pages from this sketchbook are shown as a group (cat.no.64; pls.22, 23). Picasso began to make these sculptures on his return to Paris in the autumn, in collaboration with his friend the sculptor Julio González who had a welding and metalworking workshop. 'Head' 1928 (cat.no.40) is probably the first work they made together, while 'Figure' 1931 (cat.no.41) is a playful piece made by Picasso alone.

In the early 1930s the tumescent drawings begin to reflect the features of Picasso's new love, the very young Marie-Thérèse Walter – she was seventeen when he first met her in January 1927. In 1933 and 1934 Picasso created a series of forty-six etchings on the theme of 'The Sculptor's Studio'. These eventually formed part of the great album of one hundred etchings known as the 'Vollard Suite'. In them a classical sculptor is shown in his studio with a beautiful model, the pair being a thin disguise for Picasso and Marie-Thérèse (cat.no.68i–vi; pls.24, 25).

A sometimes savage eroticism is present in drawings of this time as in the copulating 'Bathers' of 1933 (cat.no.70; pl.26). In contrast is the wonderfully jokey drawing of the same year in which a classical painted nude confronts her surrealistic sculptured counterpart in 'The Studio' (cat.no.66; pl.27). The 'sculpture' in this drawing is in fact the painted 'Seated Nude' completed by Picasso two days earlier (cat.no.98; pl.40 – see next section).

This section also includes 'The Venus of Gas' (cat.no.44), a unique example of Picasso creating a sculpture from a found object – a gas ring – without any alteration.

PLATE 17
**Standing Nudes and
Study of a Foot** 1908
30 × 21.6 (cat.no.50)

PLATE 19
**Violin** 1912
57.8 × 45.7 (cat.no.54)

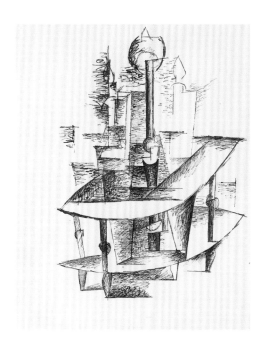

PLATE 18
**Still Life: The Cruet Set** 1911
31.4 × 24.4 (cat.no.53)

PLATE 20
**Three Nudes by the Sea** 1921
24.2 × 30.1 (cat.no.62)

PLATE 21
**Bathers (Study for a Monument)**
1928 30.2 × 22 (cat.no.63)

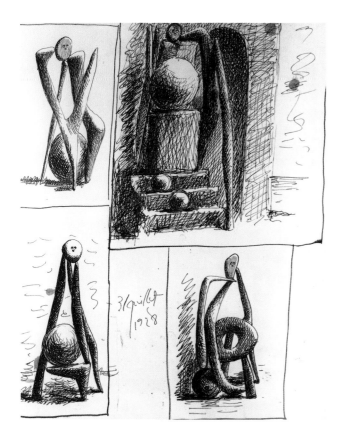

PLATE 22
**Sketchbook 1044** 1928
96.5 × 78.7 (cat.no.64)
page 8

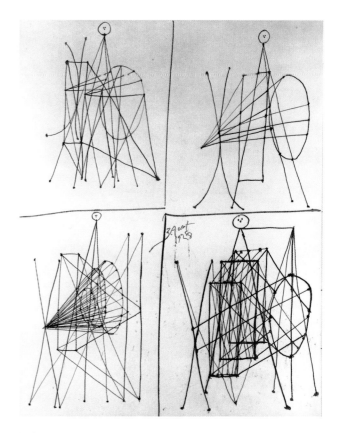

PLATE 23
**Sketchbook 1044** 1928
96.5 × 78.7 (cat.no.64)
page 20

PLATE 24
**The Vollard Suite: Sculptor,
Seated Model and Sculpted Head**
23 March 1933
26.9 × 19.4 (cat.no.68i)

PLATE 25
**The Vollard Suite: Sculptor at
Rest with a Sculpture of a Centaur
and a Woman** 31 March 1933
19.4 × 26.8 (cat.no.68iv)

PLATE 26
**Bathers** 1933
22.9 × 28.9 (cat.no.70)

PLATE 27
**The Studio** 1933
26.2 × 34.3 (cat.no.66)

# 4  Classicism and Metamorphosis

This section focuses on Picasso's sculpture and painting of the period 1927–33. The major developments in his sculpture during these years were heralded in the drawings seen in the previous section and in an important painting discussed below.

In 1928 Picasso made the first sculptures that relate to the bizarre, bulbous or bone-like figures that people his art from 1927–33. They were two closely related pieces both titled by him 'Metamorphosis'. The first is in the exhibition (cat.no.73; pl.28). The title refers to the radical transformation, or metamorphosis, of the human figure in these works. Such figures by Picasso are often referred to generically as 'metamorphic' and are also often described as 'biomorphic'. This means that the forms of the figures, while highly abstracted, nevertheless suggest, refer to, or evoke parts of the body. There is no doubt that in his works of this kind Picasso reveals an obsession with male genitalia to the extent that his female figures often take on their forms. In 'Metamorphosis I' for example, the head of the woman suggests a penis (the nose) flanked by testicles, and the smaller of the two legs is also distinctly phallic.

There is a gap between the two 'Metamorphosis' sculptures of early 1928 and an important group of metamorphic sculptures and paintings that Picasso produced from 1931–3. In this time Picasso began to explore the other new sculptural concept that had appeared first in a painting, 'The Studio' 1927–8 (cat.no.88), and then in his sketchbook drawings done at Dinard in the summer of 1928. This new concept was of sculpture as an open linear structure (see p.28). 'The Studio' is one of Picasso's grandest paintings of this period. In it an artist, depicted in linear style, confronts a sculptured head in the same manner. About a year later Picasso painted a counterpart to it, also titled 'The Studio' (cat.no.90; pl.29). Here the head has become savage, metamorphic and female, and aggressively confronts the artist. On the right a shadowy, naturalistic figure, Picasso himself, observes. His marriage to Olga was becoming increasingly unhappy at this time and the painting may reflect their conflict.

On his return to Paris in the autumn of 1928 Picasso began to make this new kind of sculpture in collaboration with his old friend the sculptor Julio González, who was a trained metalworker and had a workshop in the rue de Médéah. They made four wire constructions which were maquettes for the memorial to Apollinaire that Picasso had been commissioned to make (see pp.27–8). They were rejected by the memorial committee. In 1962 Picasso made

Picasso's sculpture studio,
Château de Boisgeloup, Gisors 1932
Photo: Brassaï © Gilberte Brassaï

two enlargements from them (cat.nos.74, 75; pl.30) and in 1972, just before his death, supervised the making of an enlargement of one of them on the scale he originally envisaged. This version, four metres high, was made for the sculpture garden of the Museum of Modern Art, New York.

'Head of a Man' 1930 (cat.no.76) is another abortive project for the monument to Apollinaire. Drawings indicate that Picasso intended it to be part of an aggressively sexualised, god-like figure, but the body was never made. In 1929–30 Picasso produced his final response to the Apollinaire commission: one of his most brilliant and magical sculptures, 'Woman in a Garden'; it was also rejected. Two versions were made; the first, in forged scrap iron, was painted white. It was kept by Picasso and is now in the Picasso Museum in Paris. Immediately on its completion Picasso commissioned González to make a version in bronze so it could be shown out-of-doors. This is the one shown here (cat.no.83; pl.31). It is not a cast; it was made from beaten and forged bronze and took González a year to complete. Picasso then installed it in his garden at Boisgeloup. Picasso's open-work wrought iron sculptures are acknowledged as works of startling originality, that broke new ground and had enormous influence on subsequent sculpture.

The most extraordinary examples of Picasso's vision of the female in terms of the male occur in the great series of 'metamorphic' heads of Marie-Thérèse Walter (see p.28) that Picasso made in the early 1930s at the Château de Boisgeloup near Gisors, not far from Paris. Picasso bought this seventeenth-century manor house in 1930, quite possibly as a hideaway where he could be with Marie-Thérèse, and work, away from his wife Olga. In the group of these sculptures assembled here the whole process of metamorphosis can be traced, beginning with a neo-classical plaster relief 'Head of a Woman and Profile' (cat.no.80) and the serenely beautiful 'Head of a Woman (Marie-Thérèse)' (cat.no.81; pl.32). But in 'Head of a Woman' (cat.no.77; pl.33) the smooth forms of Marie-Thérèse's hair have joined with her nose to create a single swollen phallic object. Then, in 'Head of a Woman' (cat.no.79; pl.34) the head is reduced simply to a collection of sexual parts: the nose and face become a penis and scrotum, the hair a long curving phallus. Finally, Picasso appears to have taken one of these heads at an early stage of its evolution and transformed it into that symbol of male sexuality 'The Cock' (cat.no.86; pl.35). The head becomes the body, the nose the left wing. In some of the metamorphic sculptures Picasso simply exaggerates elements of the female anatomy in a manner reminiscent of prehistoric figures such as the celebrated 'Venus of Lespugue', of which Picasso owned two plaster casts. These figures were thought to be fertility idols. The two bronze bathers (cat.nos.82, 85; pl.36) are examples, particularly no.85.

Picasso's metamorphic and biomorphic fantasies of women appear in his painting in a whole series of canvases of beach scenes (cat.nos.89, 92, 94, 96–8;

pls.38, 37, 39, 40). The mood ranges from savage to lyrical: in 'Figures by the Sea' 1932 (cat.no.94; pl.37) two figures blend in an embrace to form a monstrous female, her mouth also a toothed *vagina dentata*, bestriding a beach hut. Less savage, if equally monstrous, is the phallic 'Head' (cat.no.92; pl.38). This head, on its body that we do not see, is in the clouds, suggesting a sculptural monument on gigantic scale. On the other hand 'Reclining Nude' 1932 (cat.no.96; pl.39) is one of many works in which Picasso represents Marie-Thérèse as a delightful system of sensuous curves. The image here is plainly orgasmic, but Marie-Thérèse appears again, this time once more in classical calm, as a sculpted head in the painting 'Still Life: Bust, Bowl and Palette' 1932 (cat.no.95). In 'Seated Nude' 1933 (cat.no.98; pl.40) classical calm and monumentality are combined with one of Picasso's most fantastic metamorphic figures, its hunched and bulging forms particularly reminiscent of prehistoric fertility figures.

PLATE 28
**Metamorphosis I** 1928
22.8 × 18.3 × 11 (cat.no.73)

PLATE 29
**The Studio** 1928–9
162 × 130 (cat.no.90)

PLATE 30
**Figure: Project for a Monument to
Guillaume Apollinaire** 1928/*c*.1962
198 × 159.4 × 72.3 (cat.no.75)

PLATE 31
**Woman in a Garden** 1931–2
210 × 117 × 82 (cat.no.83)

PLATE 32
Head of a Woman
(Marie-Thérèse) 1931
50 × 31 × 27 (cat.no.81)

PLATE 33
Head of a Woman 1931
86 × 32 × 48.5 (cat.no.77)

PLATE 34
**Head of Woman** 1931
71.5 × 41 × 33
(cat.no.79)

PLATE 35
**The Cock** 1932
65.1 × 54.3 × 31.8
(cat.no.86)

PLATE 36
**Bather** 1931 or 1932
56 × 28.5 × 20.5
(cat.no.85)

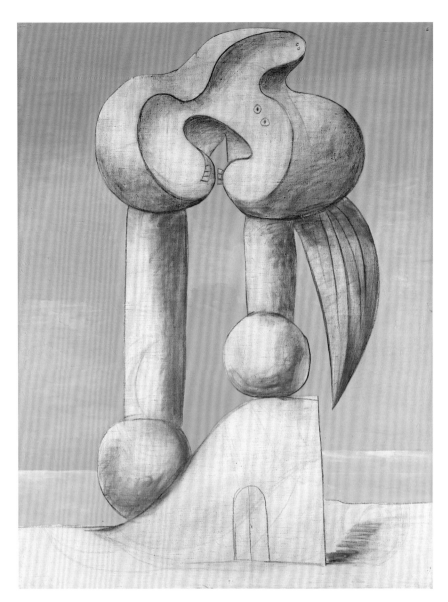

PLATE 37
**Figures by the Sea** 1932
130 × 97 (cat.no.94)

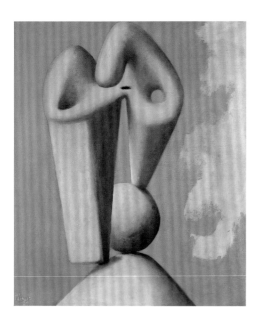

PLATE 38
**Head: Study for a
Monument** 1929
73 × 59.7  (cat.no.92)

PLATE 39
**Reclining Nude** 1932
130 × 161  (cat.no.96)

PLATE 40
**Seated Nude** 1933
130 × 97 (cat.no.98)

# 5  Death and Transformation

This section looks at Picasso's sculpture in the period from 1933 to 1947. This includes both the Spanish Civil War and the Second World War and its aftermath. Not surprisingly themes of death and the renewal of life became commonplace in Picasso's art. A new mood can already be seen in the last major sculpture at Boisgeloup, 'The Woman with a Vase' (cat.no.99; pl.42). She has been described as 'a faceless Neolithic goddess'. When Picasso died in 1973 it was a bronze cast of this work which was placed on his grave as a monument.

In 1937 Picasso acquired a vast new studio in Paris, in the rue des Grands-Augustins, and it was here that most of the sculpture of this phase was made. An important formal development was his use of found objects and textures as elements in his sculpture. Of course, he had used such things in his Cubist collages and constructions, but there they had always retained their own identity. In some cases they even represented themselves, for example the tablecloth fringe in 'Still Life' 1914 (cat.no.22; pl.11). Now, however, Picasso began to use found elements to represent other things – parts of the body usually – transforming them by some kind of magic, it seems, into vivid images.

This development is already present in two works of 1933, 'Woman Leaning on her Elbow' and 'The Orator' (cat.nos.100, 101). The first was originally modelled largely from corrugated cardboard, representing her classical draperies. This effect is also used in 'The Orator', as well as chicken wire for the torso and a found disc for the head.

Picasso's most famous found object sculpture is undoubtedly the 'Bull's Head' of 1942 made from a bicycle saddle and handlebars roughly soldered together (cat.no.103; pl.41). The effect is more of a skull than a head and Picasso once said that he saw the parts on his way to a funeral, thought about them during the service, and picked them up on the way home. If this was true (and it may not be – Picasso gave other accounts), the funeral could have been that of Julio González whose death in March 1942 affected Picasso deeply. Even if it is not strictly true, it seems that 'Bull's Head' was closely asssociated with González for Picasso. In April 1942 he painted three still lifes of a steer's skull. These were in homage to González, and one of them is included here (cat.no.112). But they also take their place among the dozens of paintings and drawings of skulls which appear in Picasso's work from the outbreak of the war, reflecting the agony of the times and the death that he now sensed all about him.

Picasso's studio, rue des
Grands-Augustins, Paris 1943
Photo: Brassaï © Gilberte Brassaï

Also during the Occupation Picasso made 'Death's Head' (cat.no.102; pl.43), considered by many to be one of his greatest sculptures. For this work he returned to traditional modelling in plaster for casting in bronze. It is not simply a skull, but a head in death with the skull beginning to show through the decaying flesh. Its presence is enhanced by its slightly larger than life scale. In 1943 Picasso made another of his most celebrated sculptures, modelled in clay, 'The Man with a Sheep' (cat.no.105; pl.44). It has been widely interpreted as an image of Christ the Good Shepherd or, equally, as an image of ideal pastoral existence, and seen as a counterpart to the pessimism of 'Death's Head', offering a message of hope and renewal in the dark days of the Occupation. Picasso denied any specifically religious reading, saying 'It's merely beautiful … In it I have expressed a human feeling, a feeling that exists now as it has always existed'. What is certain is that more than any other work 'The Man with a Sheep' established Picasso's fame as a sculptor when his work in this medium became widely known.

In the same year Picasso used found objects as the basis for another major sculpture, 'The Woman in a Long Dress' (cat.no.104; pl.45), a near life-size female figure. He saw a turn-of-the-century tailor's dummy in the Paris flea market, was struck by its 'marvellously sculpted' form and bought it. He added a wooden arm from a piece of tribal art, modelled the other arm, and added a head probably modelled by him the year before. The whole thing was cast in bronze soon after it was made. This was frequently Picasso's practice with his found object sculptures, the casting giving both visual unity and permanence to the work. Because of the fragility of Picasso's plaster and found object works it is the bronze versions which have usually been included in this exhibition.

But death was never far from Picasso's thoughts. In July 1943 he painted 'Bust of a Woman against a Grey Ground' (cat.no.113; pl.46). This is one of his grimmest and starkest evocations of the spectre of fear and death during the Occupation. The woman's features recall those of Dora Maar, his lover since 1936, although he continued his relationship with Marie-Thérèse. This painting, and 'Head of a Woman with Two Profiles' (cat.no.111; pl.47), dating from the outbreak of the war, are typical of the tortured images of Dora that Picasso produced in the course of their often stormy relationship. But as well as expressing his personal feelings he has clearly used her too as a vehicle for his wider feelings about the war. The skull-like head of 'Bust of a Woman against a Grey Ground' also echoes the gaunt muzzle of Picasso's Afghan hound Kazbek.

Picasso spent the whole of the German occupation of Paris firmly in his studio in the rue des Grands-Augustins, where he became something of a symbol of resistance. His output of sculpture during this period is remarkable in view of the difficulty of obtaining materials, and of life generally. Even more remarkable is that he was able to get a number of works cast in bronze.

Sometime soon after the war, between 1945 and 1947, Picasso produced the painting 'Monument to the Spanish Dead' (cat.no.114). It was a personal tribute to his fellow Spaniards who died fighting for France and remained in Picasso's hands until his death. It was later given to the Spanish nation.

From 1946 Picasso began to spend an increasing amount of time in the South of France and in that year established a new relationship, with Françoise Gilot, replacing Dora Maar. Shortly after, in May 1946, he encapsulated his vision of Françoise in the famous painting 'Woman-Flower' (cat.no.115; pl.48). This abstract and symbolic portrait began with Picasso asking Françoise to pose nude. He then observed her intently for an hour without making any drawing and told her to get dressed. The next day he began work from memory. The implications of growth and fertility in this work look forward to Françoise's pregnancies to come. The forms of 'Woman-Flower' have obvious affinities with those of the sculpture 'Pregnant Woman' 1949 (cat.no.106; pl.49), which commemorates the birth of Paloma, Françoise's second child by Picasso. Originally, before casting in bronze, an assemblage of plaster and iron, it has clear overtones of a tribal fetish. The following year Picasso made another, more naturalistic pregnant woman (cat.no.108; pl.50). The figure was built up in plaster over a large pot for the belly and two small pottery jars for the breasts. Françoise Gilot said that the sculpture was not only inspired by her two recent pregnancies, but represented Picasso's wish, which she had refused, that she become pregnant again.

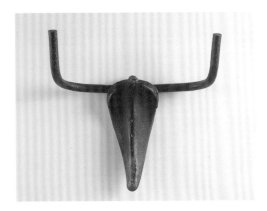

PLATE 41
**Bull's Head** 1942
42 × 41 × 15 (cat.no.103)

PLATE 42
**The Woman with a Vase** 1933
219 × 122 × 110 (cat.no.99)

PLATE 43
**Death's Head** ?1941
25 × 21 × 32 (cat.no.102)

PLATE 44
**The Man with a Sheep** 1943
222.5 × 78 × 78 (cat.no.105)

PLATE 45
**The Woman in a
Long Dress** 1943
161.3 × 54.6 × 45.7
(cat.no.104)

PLATE 46
**Bust of a Woman against
a Grey Ground** 1943
116 × 89 (cat.no.113)

PLATE 47
**Head of a Woman with
Two Profiles** 1939
92 × 73 (cat.no.111)

PLATE 48
**Woman-Flower** 1946
146 × 89 (cat.no.115)

PLATE 49
**Pregnant Woman** 1949
130 × 37 × 11.5 (cat.no.106)

PLATE 50
**The Pregnant Woman** 1950
109 × 30 × 34 (cat.no.108)

# 6  Searching in the Animal Kingdom

Picasso's love of animals was legendary and they invariably responded to him instantly. Even in his penniless early days in Paris he surrounded himself with a menagerie which included dogs, a monkey and a tame mouse. And during the war, when it was difficult to keep animals in Paris, he had an owl, some pigeons and his dog Kazbek.

He also kept cats from time to time although he disliked 'spoilt cats which sleep on sofas', preferring ones who 'chase birds, go on the razzle, roam the streets like demons'. He added that 'these free living cats are always pregnant. Obviously they think only of love.' All this amounts to a perfect description of the 'Cat and Bird' that he painted two versions of in 1939 (cat.no.131; pl.51) although it is impossible not to see it also as a reflection of the savage events in Europe which would soon turn to all-out war. In 1941 he modelled and cast in bronze another pregnant cat (cat.no.116; pl.52).

In 1948 Picasso finally settled in the South of France, with Françoise Gilot, at Vallauris, where he bought the villa La Galloise. There, animals of all kinds became part of family life and a whole sequence of memorable animal sculptures appeared. They include 'The Bull' (cat.no.117), 'The Crane' (cat.no.121; pl.53), several owls (cat.nos.122, 123; pl.54), a 'Baboon and Young' (cat.no.120; pl.55), and, most famous of all, 'The Goat' (cat.no.118; pl.56). This is one of the greatest examples of Picasso's use of found objects, combined with plaster, to create vivid images, although the child's toy cars (his son Claude's) that make up the head of the baboon are also notable. According to Françoise Gilot, Picasso had the idea for the sculpture and then set about searching the dumps of Vallauris for materials. A key element was an old wicker basket which forms the rib cage and pregnant belly of the goat. This is probably the basket that also appears in the painting 'Cock and Wicker Basket' (cat.no.132) which Picasso seems to have done before starting work on 'The Goat'. The backbone and forehead were made from an old palm branch, the horns with a section of vine, the udder from pottery jars and the vulva from a bent tin lid.

Another major sculpture of this time is 'Little Girl Skipping', also assembled from found objects bound together with plaster (cat.no.119; pl.57). Gilot said that Picasso had 'always wanted to make a sculpture that did not touch the ground. One day, watching a little girl skipping, he decided that would be the way to do it'. The base and skipping rope were made up by a local ironmonger, the body was a shallow basket, the head the lid of a chocolate box.

Picasso with still unpainted bronze cast of 'Goat's Skull and Bottle', Le Fournas, Vallauris 1952
Photo: Robert Doisneau
© Robert Doisneau/Rapho

In the same way Picasso also made a number of sculptures of still-life subjects, which he both cast in bronze and painted. 'Goat's Skull and Candle' 1951–3 (cat.no.125; pl.58) is one with a direct equivalent in a painting (cat.no.133). In the sculpture the head is made of plaster impressed with corrugated cardboard, and set with nails to represent the hair between the bicycle-handlebar horns. The painting is one of a group of four, and these works are evidence that Picasso continued to be haunted by the idea of death and the transience of life.

In the South of France, in the summer of 1946, Picasso visited the annual potters' fair at Vallauris, which had a tradition of pottery making dating back to Roman times. He was struck by the work on the stall of the Madoura pottery, met the owners and ended the day in their workshop where he made two pieces. A year later he returned and began work in earnest. He acquired a studio in the town and began a prolific production of pottery. Much of the imagery of these pieces was animal – owls, doves, fish (cat.nos.126–9; pls.59, 60). Picasso often decorated standard wares such as jugs or plates but also invented freely. In 'Fish on a Sheet of Newspaper' (cat.no.129; pl.59) the fish was carved out of a slab of wet clay. The newspaper was formed by pressing another slab of clay against a printing matrix from the Communist newspaper *Le Patriote* which was produced virtually next door to the Madoura workshop. The sheet of clay was then 'crumpled' by hand. Picasso made the egg for 'Bird Breaking Out of an Egg' (cat.no.126) by cracking open a sphere made for him by a potter. The bird was shaped from a slab of drying clay and highlighted in black paint. 'White Owl' (cat.no.127) is one of six ceramic owls all cast from a plaster model and individually painted by Picasso. But perhaps his most extraordinary ceramics are those such as 'Dove' (cat.no.128; pl.60) made from simple shapes thrown by the Madoura potters. His son Claude has vividly described this process:

'Now Jules Agar, the potter, thumping his foot on the base of his wheel to spin it, wetting his hands at regular intervals, was finishing throwing a small vase. My father grabbed it, wrung its neck, pinched it around the belly, pressed it down on the table while bending the neck. A pigeon. The hands had worked so fast, so knowingly that I had not noticed that the head had also been shaped. A pencil was picked up and a few dashes gouged the surface to indicate the eyes, the texture of the feathers. How swift and sure the hands were. So purposeful, they went directly to their business. Another day a perfectly decently boring twelve inches tall vase was turned into a head by simply bending softly the top over the belly to form a big nose.' It was, he concluded, 'magic'.

PLATE 51
**Cat and Bird** 1939
97 × 130 (cat.no.131)

PLATE 52
**The Cat** 1941
46 × 72.5 × 23
(cat.no.116)

PLATE 53
**The Crane** 1951–2
75 × 29 × 43
(cat.no.121)

PLATE 54
**Little Owl** 1951–2
33.5 × 22.5 × 19
(cat.no.123)

PLATE 55
**Baboon and Young** 1951
53 × 33 × 61 (cat.no.120)

PLATE 56
**The Goat** 1950
120.5 × 72 × 144
(cat.no.118)

PLATE 57
**Little Girl Skipping** 1950–?52
152 × 65 × 66 (cat.no.119)

PLATE 58
**Goat's Skull and Bottle** 1951–3
78.8 × 95.3 × 54.5 (cat.no.125)

PLATE 59
**Fish on a Sheet of
Newspaper** *c.*1957
39 × 32 (cat.no.129)

PLATE 60
**Dove** 1953
15 × 21 × 13
(cat.no.128)

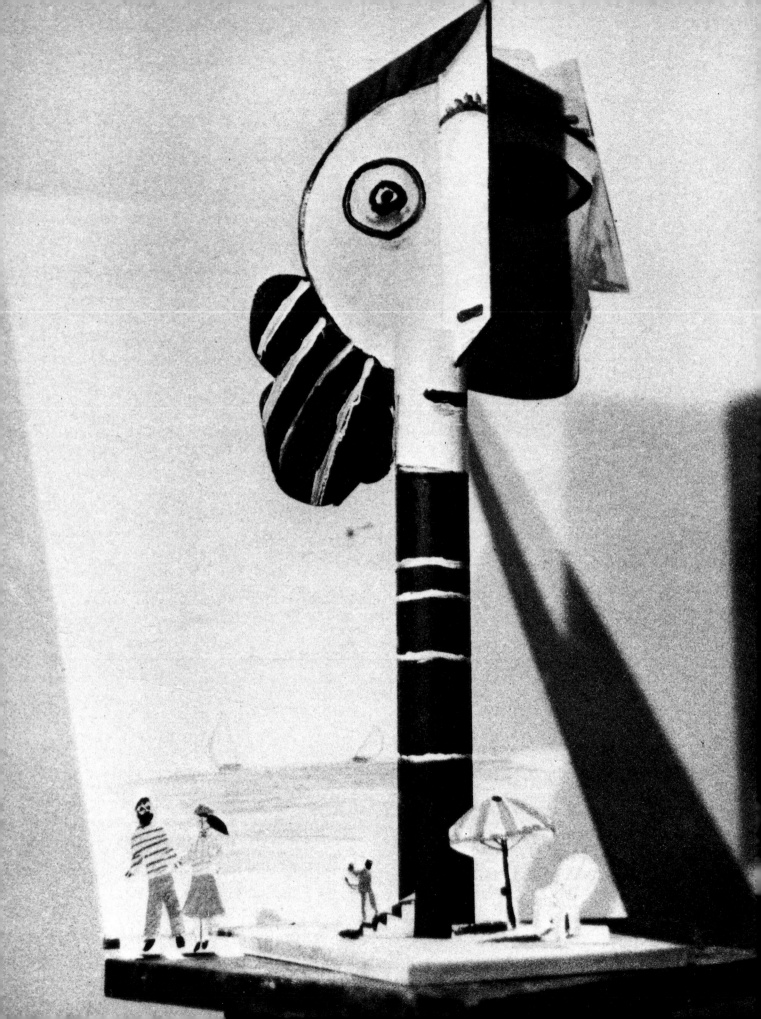

# 7 Cutting and Folding the Figure

In 1953–4 Picasso entered a new phase of sculptural activity. This coincided with the ending of his relationship with Françoise Gilot, mother of Claude (b.1947) and Paloma (b.1949). 'Woman Carrying a Child' 1953 (cat.no.135; pl.61) was probably inspired by the sight of Françoise carrying Paloma. Although playful in character it is given a certain poignancy by the knowledge that it was in the autumn of 1953 that Françoise finally left Picasso taking the children with her. Its material is scrap wood and it is one of a group of such figures Picasso made in 1957 including a whole family of dolls for Paloma. He continued to make enormously inventive constructed wooden sculpture throughout the 1950s. In 'Head' 1958 (cat.no.139; pl.63) a wooden crate is transformed by the simplest of means. 'Man' (cat.no.138; pl.62) of the same year relates to a group of drawings of artist's easels done in 1954. In the sculpture the easel is explicitly associated with the male figure and the work is perhaps an illustration of Picasso's identification of the act of painting with life itself.

As early as 1933 Picasso is on record as saying 'I should like to make sculpture in colour'. Much more than in the wooden figures he realised this ambition when, at the same time, he began to make sculptures from cut and folded sheet iron, which he then painted (cat.nos.136, 137; pl.64). These sculptures mark yet another development in Picasso's invention of new and surprising ways of representing reality in art. In them there is a constant interplay between sculptural and painterly means of representation. In their use of flat cut-out shapes to represent parts of the body they strongly call to mind Picasso's comment on his pre-Cubist paintings of 1908 that you could 'cut them up … and reassemble them' as sculpture (see p.11). Not surprisingly, his paintings of the 1950s (cat.nos.148–50; pls.65, 66) often seem to hark back to those early, enormously solid and sculptural figures. But while he continued, as always, to make paintings in which the figures looked like sculptures, his cut-out and painted figures now for the first time look like sculptures trying to be paintings.

'Head of a Woman' (cat.no.137; pl.64) was inspired by Jacqueline Roque, who came into Picasso's life as Françoise Gilot left it, and in 1961 became his second wife. Her presence is pervasive in the works of the final years of Picasso's life. Two paintings of her are included here, the 'Large Profile' 1963 (cat.no.152) and 'Woman with a Coif' 1971 (cat.no.153; pl.68). The second of these may have its origin in one of the cut and painted sculptures rather than directly in Jacqueline, but either way it is a moving example of the haunted quality that Picasso's

Mock-up for monumental enlargement of 'Head of a Woman', La Californie, Cannes 1957
Photo: David Douglas Duncan

very last paintings took on as he continued to paint in the face of approaching death.

In 1960 Picasso was able to make a great step forward in the production of his cut metal sculpures when he began a collaboration with Lionel Prejger, the owner of a metalworking factory in Vallauris. Picasso sent paper or cardboard models to the factory where they were made up in metal and painted white. Picasso then painted some pieces himself.

Prejger recalled of their agreement: 'Next day he sent us a first paper form in the shape of a superb-looking eagle. We executed the sculpture immediately, and following that, every day, other subjects were born out of his magic scissors and his inexhaustible imagination' (cat.nos.140–5; pls.67, 69, 70). Outstanding among these works is the monumental 'Woman with Outstretched Arms' of 1961 (cat.no.144; pl.70). This figure of a female bather is 1.78 metres tall, nearly six feet, and almost as wide, giving her a striking presence. Picasso has ingeniously used metal grille, painted black, to represent both her pubic hair and the areas of shadow behind her head and elsewhere.

Picasso dreamed of enlarging his sculptures to an immense size, and in 1957 he met the Norwegian sculptor Carl Nesjar who had developed a technique using concrete for making large-scale murals or three-dimensional work. The result was a number of murals and sculptures, one of which was an enlargement in concrete of 'Woman with Outstretched Arms', done in 1962 for Picasso's dealer Daniel-Henry Kahnweiler. It was placed in his garden and is five and a half metres high.

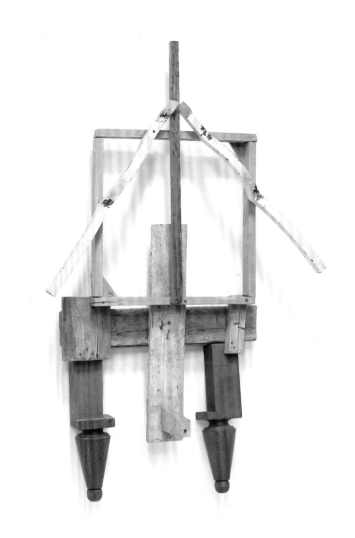

PLATE 62
**Man** 1958
117 × 76 × 25
(cat.no.138)

PLATE 61
**Woman Carrying a Child** 1953
173 × 54 × 35 (cat.no.135)

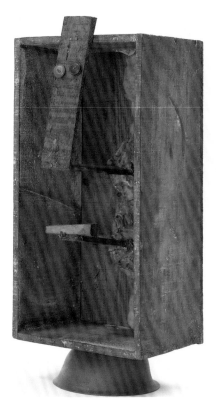

PLATE 63
**Head** 1958
50.5 × 22.2 × 20.3
(cat.no.139)

PLATE 64
**Head of a Woman** 1957
77 × 35 × 25.7
(cat.no.137)

PLATE 65
**Composition: Two Women** 1958
194.5 × 260.5 (cat.no.149)

PLATE 66
**Seated Nude** 1959
146 × 114 (cat.no.150)

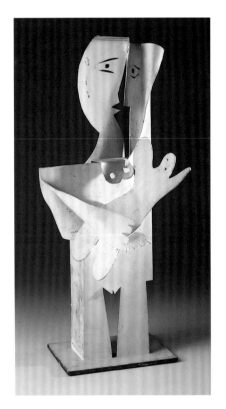

PLATE 67
**Woman and Child** 1961
43 × 17.6 × 21 (cat.no.142)

PLATE 68
**Woman with a Coif** 1971
81 × 65 (cat.no.153)

PLATE 69
**Woman in a Hat** 1961–3
126 × 73 × 41 (cat.no.145)

PLATE 70
**Woman with
Outstretched Arms** 1961
178.8 × 156.5 × 72.7
(cat.no.144)

# 8 New Arcadias

The end of Picasso's relationship with Françoise Gilot and the beginning of that with Jacqueline Roque marked a new phase in his painting as well as in his sculpture. From 1954 he embarked on a succession of series of paintings which were meditations on, and confrontations with, some of the great masterpieces of the past that had particular significance for him. First he executed a group of variations on 'The Women of Algiers' by Delacroix, a scene of sensual languor in which one of the figures becomes Jacqueline. In 1957 came more than forty paintings based on Valázquez's 'Las Meninas'. Then, between 1959 and 1962 he made over a hundred variations on Manet's 'Le Déjeuner sur l'herbe', one of the great milestones in modern art. In his versions Picasso develops Manet's original, with its clash of urban and pastoral imagery, into a much purer vision of Arcadia – an ideal pastoral existence (cat.nos.165–8; pls.71, 73). All the figures, rather than only one, become nude and one of the males is eliminated to leave the other, perhaps the artist himself, in solitary dialogue with the nude female bathers. The particular flat character of the figures in these paintings suggests that they owe something to Picasso's cut-out metal sculptures, but the paintings in turn fed the sculpture. The great 'Woman with Outstretched Arms' of 1961 (cat.no.144; pl.70) might have stepped out of one of these Arcadian scenes, for example. Then, in August 1962, Picasso made a series of eighteen maquettes in cut and folded cardboard which are transpositions into sculpture of Manet's figures (cat.nos.156–64; pls.72, 74). Through the initiative of Pontus Hulton, Director of the Moderna Museet in Stockholm, and with the collaboration of Carl Nesjar (see p.66), four of these were executed in concrete on a scale of three to four metres high and installed in the museum's sculpture garden in 1966.

Picasso with a maquette for
'Le Déjeuner sur l'herbe', Mas
Notre-Dame-de-Vie, Mougins 1964
Photo: Carl Nesjar

PLATE 71
**Le Déjeuner sur l'herbe,
after Manet** 1960
130 × 195 (cat.no.165)

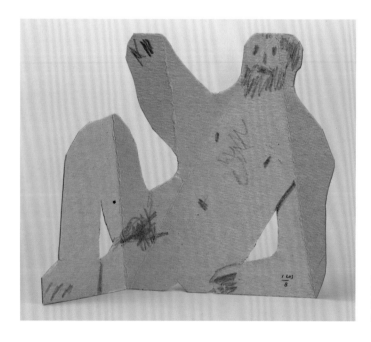

PLATE 72
**Le Déjeuner sur l'herbe: Seated
Man Leaning on his Elbow** 1962
21.5 × 26 (cat.no.161)

PLATE 73
**Le Déjeuner sur l'herbe,**
**after Manet** 1961
114 × 146 (cat.no.166)

PLATE 74
**Le Déjeuner sur l'herbe:**
**Seated Woman** 1962
34.5 × 25 (cat.no.156)

# List of Works

Measurements are given in centimetres, height before width before depth.

## 1 Crisis and Analysis

### SCULPTURES

1   **Head of a Woman (Fernande)** 1906
Tête de femme (Fernande)
Bronze 36 × 24 × 23
*Musée d'Art Moderne de la Ville de Paris*
Illustrated on page 13

2   **Woman Combing her Hair** 1906
Femme se coiffant
Bronze 41.6 × 26 × 31.4
*The Baltimore Museum of Art. The Cone Collection, formed by Dr Claribel Cone and Miss Etta Cone of Baltimore, Maryland 1950*

3   **Standing Man** 1907 or 1908
Homme debout
Painted wood 37 × 6 × 6
*Private Collection*
Illustrated on p.15

4   **Figure** ?1908
Oak with painted highlights
80.5 × 24 × 20.8
*Musée Picasso, Paris*
Illustrated on p.15

5   **Head of a Woman (Fernande)** 1909
Tête de femme (Fernande)
Plaster 40.5 × 23 × 26
*From the Envoy and Latner Family Collection*

6   **Head of a Woman (Fernande)** 1909
Tête de femme (Fernande)
Bronze 41.9 × 26.1 × 26.7
*Art Gallery of Ontario, Toronto. Purchase 1949*
Illustrated on p.17

### PAINTINGS AND DRAWINGS

7   **Study for 'Woman Combing her Hair'** 1906
Etude pour 'Femme se coiffant'
Pencil on laid paper 31 × 22.5
*Klaus Hegewisch, Hamburg*

8   **Head and Figure Studies** 1906
Etude de nus
Conté crayon on paper
64.8 × 47.9
*Museum of Fine Arts, Boston. Arthur Tracy Cabot Fund 1963*

9   **Two Nudes** 1906
Deux femmes nues
Oil on canvas 151.3 × 93
*The Museum of Modern Art, New York. Gift of G. David Thompson in honour of Alfred H. Barr, Jr 1959*
Illustrated on p.14

10   **Seated Nude with Crossed Legs** 1906
Femme nue assise les jambes croisées
Oil on canvas 151 × 100
*Národní Galerie, Prague*
Illustrated on p.14

11   **Nude with Raised Arms** 1908
Nu aux bras levés de profil
Oil on wood 67 × 27
*Private Collection*

12   **Standing Nude** 1908
Nu debout de face
Oil on wood 67 × 27
*Private Collection*

13   **Seated Nude** 1908
Femme nue assise
Oil on canvas 150 × 100
*The State Hermitage Museum, St Petersburg*
Illustrated on p.16

14   **Head and Shoulders of the Farmer's Wife** 1908
Buste de la fermière
Oil on canvas 81 × 65
*The State Hermitage Museum, St Petersburg*

15   **Study for 'Head of a Woman (Fernande)'** 1909
Etude pour 'Tête de femme (Fernande)'
Charcoal with chalk highlights on paper 62.8 × 48
*Musée Picasso, Paris*

16   **Head and Shoulders of a Woman (Fernande)** 1909
Buste de femme (Fernande)
Oil on canvas 60.6 × 51.3
*Art Institute of Chicago. The Joseph Winterbotham Collection 1940*

17   **Seated Woman** 1909
Femme assise
Oil on canvas 81 × 65
*Private Collection*
Illustrated on p.17

18   **Bust of a Woman** 1909–10
Buste de femme
Oil on canvas 73 × 60
*Musée National d'Art Moderne, Centre Georges Pompidou, Paris. Donation Louise et Michel Leiris 1984*

## 2 Construction and Synthesis

### SCULPTURES

19   **Guitar** ?1912–13
Guitare
Sheet metal and wire
77.5 × 35 × 19.3
*The Museum of Modern Art, New York. Gift of the Artist 1971*
Illustrated on p.21

20   **Guitarist with Sheet Music** 1913
Guitariste avec partition
Paper construction 22 × 10.5
*Private Collection*

21   **Glass and Dice** 1914
Verre et dé
Painted wood 23.5 × 21.6 × 7
*Private Collection*

22   **Still Life** 1914
Nature morte
Painted wood with upholstery fringe 25.4 × 45.7 × 9.2
*Tate Gallery. Purchased 1969*
Illustrated on p.22

23   **Glass of Absinthe** 1914
Verre d'absinthe
Sand-covered bronze and silver-plated spoon 21.5 × 16.5 × 6.5
*Musée National d'Art Moderne, Centre Georges Pompidou, Paris. Donation Louise et Michel Leiris 1984*

24   **Glass of Absinthe** 1914
Verre d'absinthe
Painted bronze and silver-plated spoon 22 × 16.5 × 5
*The Berggruen Collection on loan to the National Gallery, London*
Illustrated on p.23

25   **Bottle of Bass, Glass and Newspaper** 1914
Bouteille de Bass, verre et journal
Painted tin, sand, wire and paper
20.7 × 14 × 8.5
*Musée Picasso, Paris*

26   **Violin** 1915
Violon
Painted sheet iron and wire
100 × 63 × 18
*Musée Picasso, Paris*
Illustrated on p.24

### PAINTINGS AND COLLAGES

27   **Musical Score and Guitar** 1912
Feuille de musique et guitare
Papier collé and pins on cardboard 42.5 × 48
*Musée National d'Art Moderne, Centre Georges Pompidou, Paris. Legs de M. Georges Salles 1967*
Illustrated on p.21

28   **Glass, Guitar and Bottle** 1913
Verre, guitare, bouteille
Oil, papier collé, gesso and pencil on canvas 65.4 × 53.6
*The Museum of Modern Art, New York. The Sidney and Harriet Janis Collection 1967*

29   **Violin, Glass and Bottle** 1913
Violon au café
Oil on canvas 81 × 54
*A. Rosengart*

30   **Head of a Girl** 1913
Tête de jeune fille
Oil on canvas 55 × 38
*Musée National d'Art Moderne, Centre Georges Pompidou, Paris. Donation de M. Henri Laugier 1963*

31   **Wineglass with Slice of Lemon** c.1914
Verre avec tranche de citron
Oil on canvas 20.5 × 18.5
*Royal Museum of Fine Arts, Copenhagen*

32   **Woman with a Mandolin** 1914
Femme à la mandoline
Oil, sand and charcoal on canvas
115.5 × 47.5
*The Museum of Modern Art, New York. Gift of David Rockefeller 1975*

112 **Still life with a Steer's Skull**
1942
Nature morte au crâne de boeuf
Oil on canvas 117 × 89
*Pinacoteca di Brera, Milan.*
*Donazione Emilio e Maria Jesi*

113 **Bust of a Woman against a Grey Ground** 1943
Buste de femme
Oil on canvas 116 × 89
*Marx Collection on permanent loan to the Nationalgalerie, Berlin*
Illustrated on p.53

114 **Monument to the Spanish Dead** 1945–7
Monument aux Espagnols morts pour la France
Oil on canvas 195 × 130
*Museo Nacional Centro de Arte Reina Sofía, Madrid*

115 **Woman-Flower** 1946
Femme-fleur
Oil on canvas 146 × 89
*Private Collection. Courtesy Thomas Ammann Fine Art, Zurich*
Illustrated on p.54

## 6  Searching in the Animal Kingdom

SCULPTURES

116 **The Cat** 1941
Le Chat
Bronze 46 × 72.5 × 23
*Private Collection*
Illustrated on p.59

117 **The Bull** 1949 or 1950
Le Taureau
Bronze 40 × 66 × 21.5
*Private Collection*

118 **The Goat** 1950
La Chèvre
Bronze 120.5 × 72 × 144
*Musée Picasso, Paris*
Illustrated on p.61

119 **Little Girl Skipping** 1950–?52
Petite Fille sautant à la corde
Bronze 152 × 65 × 66
*Mr and Mrs Rafael Lopez Cambil*
Illustrated on p.62

120 **Baboon and Young** 1951
La Guenon et son petit
Bronze 53 × 33 × 61
*Private Collection*
Illustrated on p.61

121 **The Crane** 1951–2
La Grue
Painted bronze 75 × 29 × 43
*The Berggruen Collection on loan to the National Gallery, London*
Illustrated on p.60

122 **Little Owl** 1951–2
Petite Chouette
Painted bronze 26 × 18.7 × 14.6
*Hirshhorn Museum and Sculpture Garden, Smithsonian Institution, Washington. Gift of Joseph H. Hirshhorn 1966*

123 **Little Owl** 1951–2
Petite Chouette
Plaster, screws, nails and metal objects 33.5 × 22.5 × 19
*Marina Picasso. Courtesy Jan Krugier Gallery, New York*
Illustrated on p.60

124 **Still Life: Pitcher and Figs** 1951–2
Nature morte: Broc et figues
Plaster, wood and iron
32 × 48.5 × 21.5
*Marina Picasso. Courtesy Jan Krugier Gallery, New York*

125 **Goat's Skull and Bottle** 1951–3
Crâne de chèvre, bouteille et bougie
Painted bronze
78.8 × 95.3 × 54.5
*The Museum of Modern Art, New York. Mrs Simon Guggenheim Fund 1956*
Illustrated on p.62

126 **Bird Breaking Out of an Egg** c.1953
Oiseau sortant d'un oeuf
Ceramic 43 × 33 × 25.5
*Mr and Mrs Rafael Lopez Cambil*

127 **White Owl** 1953
Hibou blanc
Ceramic 34 × 33 × 24
*Private Collection*

128 **Dove** 1953
Colombe
Ceramic 15 × 21 × 13
*Musée d'Art Moderne, Céret*
Illustrated on p.63

129 **Fish on a Sheet of Newspaper** c.1957
Poisson sur une feuille de journal
Ceramic 39 × 32
*Private Collection*
Illustrated on p.63

130 **Arm** 1959
Bras vertical
Bronze 58 high
*Moderna Museet Stockholm*

PAINTINGS

131 **Cat and Bird** 1939
Chat à l'oiseau
Oil on canvas 97 × 130
*Mrs Victor W. Ganz*
Illustrated on p.59

132 **Cock and Wicker Basket** 1950
Coq et panier d'osier
Oil on wood 116 × 89
*Marina Picasso. Courtesy Galerie Jan Krugier, Geneva*

133 **Goat's Skull, Bottle and Candle** 1952
Crâne de chèvre, bouteille et bougie
Oil on canvas 89.2 × 116.2
*Tate Gallery. Purchased 1957*

## 7  Cutting and Folding the Figure

SCULPTURES

134 **Françoise Gilot** 1950
Painted tile 100 × 21 × 10
*Private Collection*

135 **Woman Carrying a Child** 1953
Femme portant un enfant
Painted wood and section of palm leaf 173 × 54 × 35
*Private Collection*
Illustrated on p.67

136 **Head of a Woman** 1957
Tête de femme
Painted sheet iron
87 × 27.5 × 45
*Musée Picasso, Paris*

137 **Head of a Woman** 1957
Tête de femme
Painted sheet iron
77 × 35 × 25.7
*Private Collection*
Illustrated on p.68

138 **Man** 1958
Homme
Wood and nails 117 × 76 × 25
*Mr and Mrs Rafael Lopez Cambil*
Illustrated on p.67

139 **Head** 1958
Tête
Open wood box, nails, buttons, painted plaster and painted synthetic resin mounted on overturned ceramic dish
50.5 × 22.2 × 20.3
*The Museum of Modern Art, New York. Gift of Jacqueline Picasso in honour of the Museum's continuous commitment to Pablo Picasso's art, 1984*
Illustrated on p.68

140 **Standing Nude** 1960 or 1961
Femme nue debout
Painted sheet iron 42 × 30 × 21
*Private Collection*

141 **Standing Woman** 1961
Femme debout
Painted sheet iron 42 × 19 × 9
*Private Collection, Switzerland*

142 **Woman and Child** 1961
Femme et enfant
Painted sheet iron
43 × 17.6 × 21
*Private Collection*
Illustrated on p.70

143 **Woman with a Tray and a Bowl** 1961
Femme au plateau et à la sébile
Painted sheet iron 115 × 62 × 34
*Private Collection*

144 **Woman with Outstretched Arms** 1961
Femme aux bras écartés
Painted iron and metal sheeting
178.8 × 156.5 × 72.7
*The Museum of Fine Arts, Houston. Gift of the Esther Florence Whinery Goodrich Foundation*
Illustrated on p.71

145 **Woman in a Hat** 1961–3
Femme au chapeau
Painted sheet iron
126 × 73 × 41
*Beyeler Collection, Basel*
Illustrated on p.71

146 **Jacqueline with a Green Ribbon** 1962
Jacqueline au ruban vert
Sheet iron with oil paint and crayon 50.7 × 39 × 28
*Courtesy Jan Krugier Gallery, New York*

147 **Bust of a Woman** 1964
Buste de femme
Painted sheet iron 48 × 34 × 30
*Christine Ruiz-Picasso*

PAINTINGS

148 **Two Women on the Beach** 1956
Deux femmes sur la plage
Oil on canvas 195 × 260
*Musée National d'Art Moderne, Centre Georges Pompidou, Paris. Donation de Mme Paul Cuttoli 1963*

149 **Composition: Two Women** 1958
Composition: Deux femmes
Oil on canvas 194.5 × 260.5
*Museo de Arte Contemporaneo Sofia Imber, Caracas*
Illustrated on p.69

150 **Seated Nude** 1959
Nu accroupi
Oil on canvas 146 × 114
*Private Collection, Switzerland*
Illustrated on p.69

151 **Seated Woman** 1962
Femme assise
Oil on canvas 146 × 116
*Private Collection*

# Photographic Credits

Thomas Amman Fine Art
C. Bahier
Baltimore Museum of Art
Galerie Beyeler
Studio Brady
Chester Brummel
Gelett Burgess
Museo de Arte Contemporaneo
Sofia Imber, Caracas
Musée d'Art Moderne, Céret
David Douglas Duncan
Kunstsammlung Nordrhein-Westfalen,
Düsseldorf
Ursula Edelmann
Ali Elai
Städelsches Kunstinstitut Frankfurt
am Main
Vladimir Fyman
Béatrice Hatala
The Museum of Fine Arts, Houston

Imageart Antibes
Bill Jacobson
Bob Kolbrener
Galerie Jan Krugier
National Gallery, London
Robert E. Mates
Metropolitan Museum of Art,
New York
P. Migeat
Carl Nesjar
Museum of Modern Art, New York
Pace Gallery
Ellen Page Wilson
Musée National d'Art Moderne,
Centre Georges Pompidou, Paris
Photothèque des Musées de la Ville
de Paris
Service Photographique de la
Réunion des Musées Nationaux,
Paris

Philadelphia Museum of Art
Eric Pollitzer
Museo del Prado, Madrid
Národní Galerie, Prague
State Hermitage Museum,
St Petersburg
Staatsgalerie Stuttgart
Tate Gallery
Art Gallery of Ontario, Toronto
Sean Weaver

All photographs from the Musée
Picasso, Paris © RMN

The publishers have made every effort
to trace all the relevant copyright
holders and apologise for any omis-
sions that may have been made.